Hanan Amer Class 14

Alternative Nursery Rhymes

(Looney Limericks and more!)

By **Robert Taylor**

Best wishes from

Robert Taylor

Published by Dangeroo Publishing

ISBN 9780955926037, ~~£4.99~~

£5.00

Typeset & printed by The Jedburgh Press (www.jedpress.co.uk)

"I'M COMING FOR YOU MICE!"

Alternative Nursery Rhymes -
Looney Limericks and more!)

If you read the title on the front cover you may believe that this is a book for infant children – WELL IT IS NOT!
It is aimed mainly at 6 to 11 years olds!

It is a dip in, fun book, with lots of silly, short, hopefully funny poems – and lots of daft drawings too!!!

When my son Scott, was very young I began reading nursery rhymes to him as parents do. I became quite fascinated by them and not a little bit curious. Some of the rhymes seemed quite odd and unusual to say the least. I then found myself, being a little bit naughty, changing the endings and making up variations on these rhymes. Some of these I read to Scott.
One day, when he was about five, he came home from school and said to me.

"You know that poem you wrote about Hickory Dickory Dock?"

"Oh, Yes," I said. "That one!"

"Well," he said somewhat indignantly. "You've written the wrong words to it!"

"You are right," I said, laughing. "I believe I have!"

Later, I ended up with a whole book full of -the wrong words to Nursery rhymes – and here it is.

The title - "Alternative nursery rhymes (Looney Limericks and more!") just about sums up the contents of the book.

All told there are about 120 POEMS IN THIS BOOK.
Value for money, I hope.

This book is dedicated to the thousands of children and teachers who have heard me and read my poetry and stories in schools and who have laughed, cheered, smiled, clapped, joined in with – and generally had fun with poetry! That's how it should be!

All Illustrations by Robert Taylor.
Except for -

> "Mary had other animals too you know." By Joyce Worsfold.
> "The strangest thing I ever did see." By Scott Taylor.
> "All about the sausage." By Scott Taylor.
> "Incey Wincey spider." By Alison Taylor.
> Front cover by Alison Taylor.

Three other books by Robert Taylor –
PUBLISHED IN PAPERBACK BY DANGEROO PUBLISHING.

"Shark Attack (The poems are back!)." £4.99.
(80 pages. Sixty poems).

"The Angel takes flight." £4.99.
(Fantasy fiction about the Angel of the North and a little boy called Ben).

"The Goolagong Gang Stories." £6.99.
(The adventures of a boy from first school to first job).

The books can be bought or ordered at any good bookshop
Or Purchased from www. dangeroo.co.uk Tel 01830 520 344,
and Robert can be booked to perform at your school using the above contact details too.

ALTERNATIVE NURSERY RHYMES
(Looney Limericks and more!)

1. The end of time / Little Miss M.
2. Two conflicting news reports about Humpty Dumpty.
3. My old man / We've got a right one here constable.
4. Twinkle, twinkle little cow / The seaside song.
5. Young Mother Hubbard / Johnny needs attention again.
6. Three smart mice / The sleepwalker.
7. The man in the moon / According to new evidence.
8. The Grand old Duke's other march / little boy blue.
9. Round in circles / Baa! Baa! Black sheep / Mary's green fingers.
10. Mary had other animals too you know.
11. Jack was nimble / Tom's last crime.
12. On the move / Georgie Porgie met his match.
13. Little Bo Peep.
14. The rock a bye baby court case / Elsie Marley (computer nut!)
15. Doctor Foster's wrong mode of transport / Jack Horner hears singing.
16. Peter Piper's not well / Look! I've caught a big one!
17. Ice cream / Tommy Tucker can't sing.
18. Gorillas on the wall.
19. Why they really went up that hill / A lady in Tipperary.
20. The Giants revenge on Jack / Humpty Dumpty's in trouble again.
21. Old King Cole's band.
22. Rock a bye baby / One day son all this will be yours!
23. Have you any wool?
24. A stylish young man / Meanwhile in Haltwhistle / Sleeping like a top.
25. Man in Nuneaton / Slow and steady / A musical Aunt.
26. The owl and pussy didn't quite get to sea!
27. Twinkle, twinkle, my class teacher / alternate version.
28. In a minute.
29. The old names / Good, but not that good!
30. Nathaniel Knox.
31. Twinkle, twinkle funny clown.
32. A well ordered life.
33. All about the pork pie / The wing commander.
34. Bath night in Bude / My baby brother / eating out.
35. Not this man's best friend.
36. A Skye boat song / A political animal.

37. The strangest thing I ever did see / The next strangest thing.
38. All about the sausage / Jennifer Jones.
39. Unusual growth.
40. A long nose in Melrose / heavy drinking / Meanwhile in Byrness.
41. A sandwich in Nantwich / A sudden movement in the reptile pool.
42. A lady in Dunoon.
43. A tiger's advice to his keeper / A very strange tale.
44. My pet giraffe.
45. Giggle Glasses.
46. Nobody's better than me.
47. Party Animals.
48. Little frog.
49. This charming man / Guitar man.
50. Bongo banging! / Twinkle, twinkle little star.
51. Sporting horse / Sporting cow.
52. Your worst nightmare / Daredevil Toad.
53. Reverting to type / Extra! Extra! Pig swims channel.
54. Looking through windows.
55. Professor Sidney Barnacles most useless inventions (so far!)
56. Alliteration with numbers.
57. The mermaid.
58. Big Mac (The gigantic giant!)
59. A recipe to make a perfect Dragon.
60. What goes on in a cats' head.
61. The family are not at home.
62. So, what!
63. Sidney the Spider.
64. The wincey family outing.
65. When Billy got eaten by a crocodile.
66. The Lion's rap.
67. There's trouble at the zoo.
68. Seven little monkeys / A note on etiquette.
69. A meal deal.
70. A leak in the head.
71. Meanwhile - in another school / Diplodocus daydreams.
72. Amazing talent / Jumping Jellybeans – flying bulls!
73. If nobody sang.

THE END OF TIME.

Hickory dickory dock,
The elephant ran up the clock.
Just think of that?
He squashed it flat.
Tickory, tickory - SPLAT!

LITTLE MISS M.

Little Miss Muffet,
sat on her tuffet,
eating her curds and whey.
'Til they opened a burger bar,
just over the road
and now she has take away!

CONFLICTING NEWS REPORTS ABOUT HUMPTY DUMPTY.

HE'S OKAY NOW!

Humpty Dumpty sat on a wall,
Humpty Dumpty had a great fall.
But all the kingsmen knew just what to do.
It's a wonderful invention is super glue.

HE IS NO MORE!

There was a fellow named Humpty,
Who fell off the wall and went Bumpty,
There was a mighty crash,
followed by mash.
Poor old Humpty Dumpty - Bumpty!
P.S. Well, the rumour has it - he was a bad egg!

MY OLD MAN. (HE PLAYS DRUMS).

My old man, rather sadly,
He plays drums, but very badly.
With a knick knack, paddy whack.
He's sitting in his vest,
bashing on those drums.
"Oh! Give the flippin' things a rest!"

WE'VE GOT A RIGHT ONE HERE CONSTABLE!

Wee, Willie Winkie, ran through the town,
upstairs and downstairs in his nightgown.
A couple of policemen saw him;
Said - "What are you doing, hey?"
They guessed he was a nut case
and carried him away.

TWINKLE TWINKLE, LITTLE COW!

Twinkle, Twinkle, little cow,
since you jumped over that moon,
I've longed to know - how.
Did you vault with a pole,
from a skyscraper roof?
Or was a powerful rocket,
attached to each hoof?
……………..WHOOOOOSH!

THE SEASIDE SONG.

Sing a song
of sixpence,
there's dirt
in my eye,
four and twenty
seagulls,
have pooped
from the sky!
AAAHHHRGH!

YOUNG MOTHER HUBBARD.

Young Mother Hubbard
went to the cupboard,
to get the poor dog a bone.
When she got there,
The cupboard was bare,
except for a mobile phone.
She dialled for a take away.
They came in a trice.
Barbecued spare ribs
with chips and fried rice.
YUM! YUM!
P.S. And the dog
loved them too!

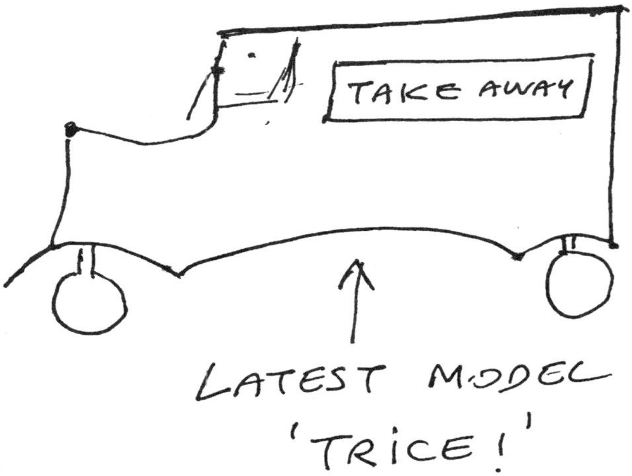

JOHNNY NEEDS ATTENTION AGAIN.

Seesaw, Margery Daw,
Johnny shall have a new plaster.
He has had, a plaster a day,
because he's a walking disaster.

THREE SMART MICE.

Three smart mice, three smart mice,
See how they hide, see how they hide.
They never run after the farmer's wife.
She's fat and she carries
a carving knife.
They wait 'til she's gone
and enjoy a good life -
three smart mice.

THE SLEEPWALKER.

Diddle, diddle, dumpling,
My son John,
When sleepwalking with no pyjamas on.
Right across the landing,
up and down the stairs,
my son John was....
HERE! THERE!
And ....BARE!

THE MAN IN THE MOON.

The man in the moon,
Looked down from the moon
And he saw class three being quiet.
Everyone was working.
Nobody was shirking.
And there was no sign of quarrel, or of riot.
The man in the moon,
stared down from the moon,
and he stared quite amazed through space.
Class three, writing lots,
With commas and full stops
And their teacher had a smile on her face!

WELL, ACCORDING TO NEW EVIDENCE.

Hey diddle, diddle,
When the cat played the fiddle,
The dog played a huge, long bassoon.
The moon jumped over the cow,
But don't ask me how,
And the dish and spoon marry in June.

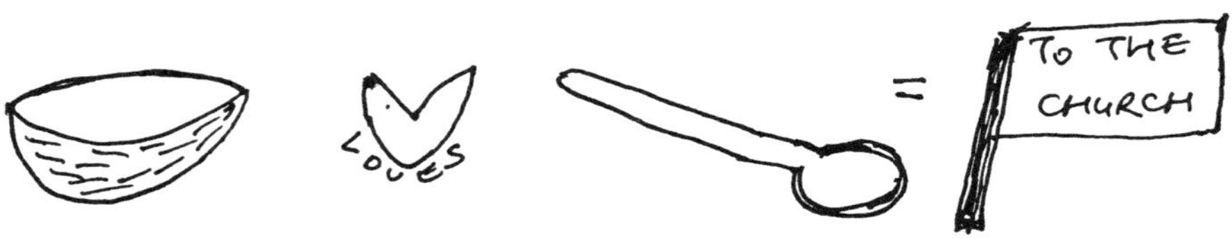

THE GRAND OLD DUKE'S OTHER MARCH.

Oh, the grand old Duke of York,
He had ten thousand men.
He marched them right through
the middle of a hill
and he marched them out again.
And when they were in,
They were dirty.
And when they were out,
They were clean.
And when they were only half way out,
Well, they didn't know where they'd been!

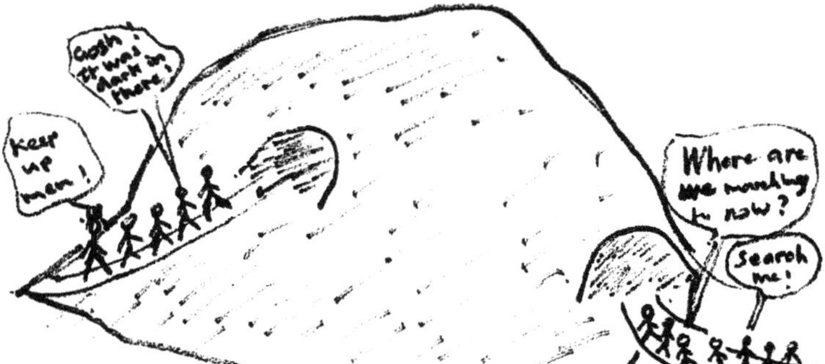

LITTLE BOY BLUE.

Little boy blue,
Come blow your horn.
The roaster has laryngitis
And it will soon be dawn!

ROUND IN CIRCLES.

Here we go round the Mulberry Bush,
The Mulberry Bush, the Mulberry Bush,
Seventeen times round the Mulberry Bush….
The driver's lost again!!!!!!

BAA! BAA! BLACK SHEEP!

"Baa! Baa! Black sheep,
Have you any wool?"
….."Wool? Wool?
Why of course I've got wool!
I'm a sheep aren't I?
For pity's sake!"

MARY'S GREEN FINGERS.

"Mary, Mary, quite contrary,
How does you garden grow?"
"Er, well……***upwards*** - mostly!"

One of the singing donkeys on his day off!

<u>MARY HAD OTHER ANIMALS TOO, YOU KNOW!</u>

Mary had a little lamb,
Her fleece was white as snow…….
But it was the three singing donkeys
and the guitar playing horse,
who really stole the show.
Hee Haw!
Hee Haw!
Hee Haw!
NEIGH!
They really stole the show!......
Twang!

JACK WAS NIMBLE.

Jack was nimble,
Jack was quick.
Jack jumped over
the candlestick.

Easy peasy!
That's not great!
Let's see how Jack manages
A ***five barred gate!***

Note - Pride comes before a fall.

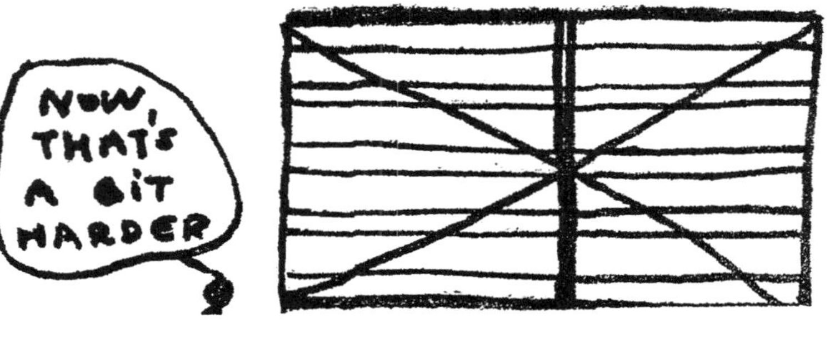

TOM'S LAST CRIME.

Tom, Tom, the piper's son,
Stole a pig and away he ran,
into the traffic and under a truck.
The piper's son was out of luck.
(But the pig got away though!)

ON THE MOVE.

There was an old woman
Who lived in a shoe,
She had so many children,
She didn't know what to do.
So, she moved to a Wellington,
on the edge of the town.
It was
TALLER
And
R O O M I E R.

A SIX UP and THREE DOWN !

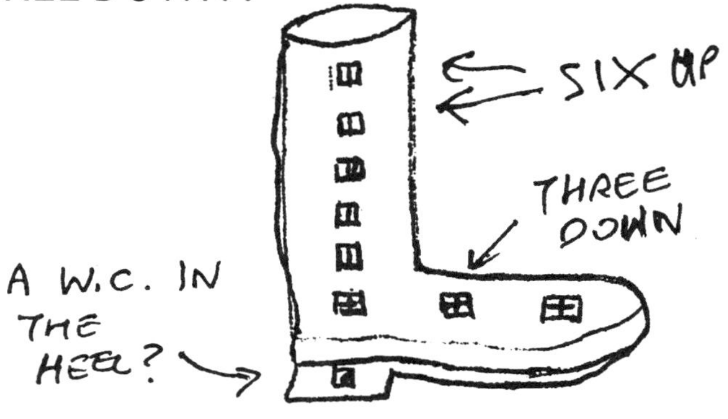

GEORGIE PORGIE MET HIS MATCH.

Georgie Porgie, pudding and pie,
kissed the girls and made them cry,
Until Sophie socked him in the eye,
So, he didn't do that know more!

LITTLE BO PEEP!

Little Bo Peep has lost her sheep
And doesn't know where to find them….
They'll be alright, oh rub a dub dub.
It's a quiz night tonight
so they're down at the pub.

"Right, sheep! What's the capital of France?!"
"Baaa!"
"No, sorry. It's Paris. Better luck next time!"
"Right, sheep, here's your next question-
What part of the pub are we now in? "
"Baaa!"
"Oh, well done, sheep! You've got that one right!"

Note – This is our local the "Rancid Ferret!" (It's seen better days!)

THE ROCK A BYE BABY COURTCASE.
(EXTRA! EXTRA! READ ALL ABOUT IT!)

Rock a bye baby, The child minder's in court,
For not leaving the baby, In the place where she ought,
She left baby and cradle, high up in a tree,
at the whims of the weather.
She seems crazy to me!

ELSIE MARLEY - COMPUTER NUT!

Elsie Marley's grown so fine.
She won't go out to feed the swine.
She play's computer games all day.
Can't talk to her, she's far away.
She just comes down for dinner or lunch
and takes it back upstairs to crunch.
You just can't reason, her mind is set,
on computer games and the internet.
What happened to mother and child relationships?
Gone to pot.
……… Blown to bits!

DOCTOR FOSTER'S WRONG MODE OF TRANSPORT.

Doctor Foster went
to Gloucester,
In a shower of rain,
Sensible folk went in by car
And you'll not hear
them complain.

JACK HORNER HEARS SINGING.

Little Jack Horner,
Sat in a corner,
eating his Christmas pie.
He put in a finger,
And pulled out a singer,
Who sung songs from the King and I!

PETER PIPER'S NOT WELL.

Peter Piper picked a pot of plums
and ate them with a friend.
Now they're sat upon the Loo
and have both been there since ten!

(Note – red wine can be thicker, but plums are quicker!)

LOOK I'VE CAUGHT A BIG ONE!

One, two three, four, five,
Once I caught a fish alive,
Six, seven, eight, nine, ten,
Then I let it go again,
Why did you let it go?
Because it was a ....
SHAAAAAAAAAAARRRRRRKKKKKKK!
.......you know.

ICE CREAM.

Ride a cock horse, to Banbury Cross,
To see an ice cream man in a kiosk.
Or out in his van, at the fair I suppose.
There'll be ice cream - ***and music!*** - wherever he goes.

TOMMY TUCKER CAN'T SING.

Little Tommy Tucker,
Sang for his supper,
But his singing was so bad.
He nearly starved poor lad.
He used to make this weird wailing sound,
while busking near the underground.
Then Tommy Tucker saw the light.
He could not sing but he was quite bright.
Now he's a manager, for ***other*** singers.
They keep him in suppers, teas and dinners!

Note - ***VERY BIG DINNERS TOO !!!!!***

GORILLAS ON THE WALL.

Two great huge gorillas
sitting on a wall.
One called Peter
and one called Paul.
"Fly away Peter! Fly away Paul!
Or just swing on a rope or something –
As your nearly – ***seven feet tall!"***

(And built like a pair of barn doors!)

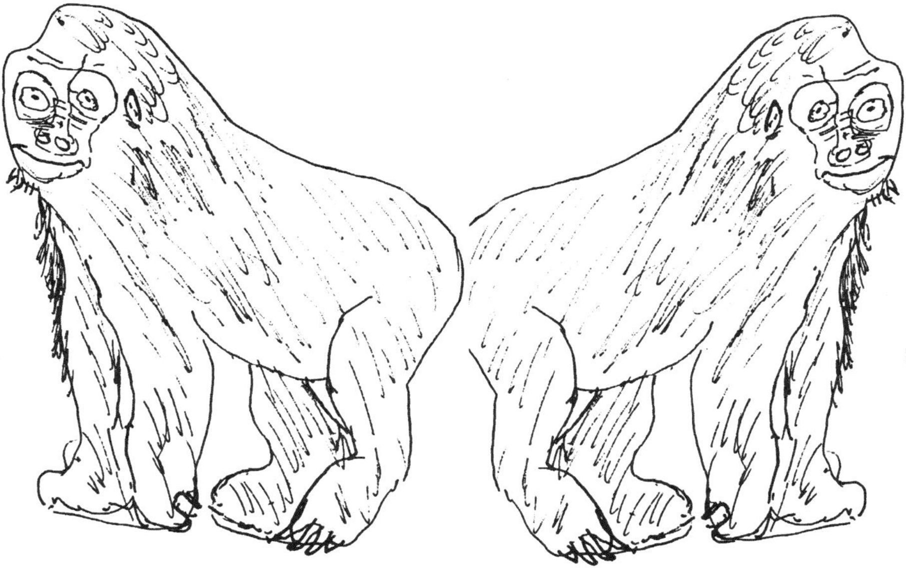

This is Peter. This is Paul.

But don't try flying or anything – now that *would* be stupid!

WHY THEY REALLY UP THAT HILL.

Jack and Jill went up the hill,
(forgot about the water).
They only went to play the game,
Jill's sister Josie, taught her!!

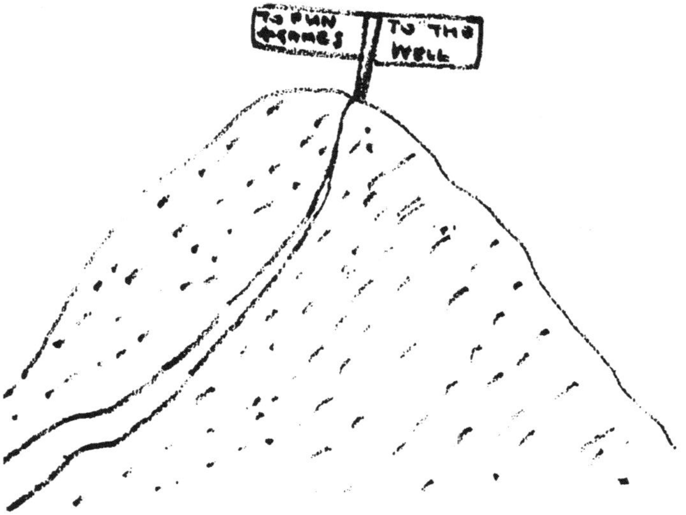

A LADY FROM TIPPERARY.

A clever young lady from Tipperary,
swallowed a large dictionary.
Now you should hear her words.
They're the longest you've heard - like.....
San-flan-dango-dipper-flipper-airy-canary!

P.S. Look that up at your peril!
It might not be in your dictionary!
(Unless you've got one like mine!)

THE GIANT'S REVENGE ON JACK.

The castle was empty.
The giant had left a sign.
There will be no more stealing
from me this time.
FEE FI FO FUM.
I'VE GONE AND MOVED TO
BIRMING- ***HUM!***

(The posh part!)

HUMPTY DUMPTY'S UPWARDS FALL.

Humpty Dumpty sat on the wall,
Humpty Dumpty had a great fall,
Down to a trampoline,
Then up to a tree.
“Get the fire brigade to rescue …..Meeeeee !”

HUMPTY DUMPTY'S SMELLY FALL.

Humpty Dumpty sat on a wall,
Humpty Dumpty had a great fall,
Down into a dung heap,
In his best clothes-es,
Now all the kingsmen are holding their noses!
Poo! Poo! Poo!

OLD KING COLE'S BAND.

Old king Cole was a merry old soul
And a merry old soul was he.
He formed this heavy metal band,
with his wife and his fiddlers three.
He and the queen were the singers,
Fiddler one, played on the drums.
Fiddler two, played guitars and keyboards
and fiddler three did all the sums!
They all had such a w - w - wonderful time,
It did not matter if they could not sing,
because you never ever get booed off stage,
when you are the queen and the king.
Ha ! Ha!
when you are the queen and the king.
Tee! Hee!
when you are the queen and the king.

"Boooo! Boooo! Booo!"

You ***hardly*** ever get booed
off stage when you are
the queen
And the king!!!!

ROCK A BYE BABY.

Rock a bye baby,
Your cradle is green.
Your father is a nobleman
And your mother is a queen.

Rock a bye baby,
Your cradle is yellow.
Why do I tell lies
my lovely young fellow.

Rock a bye baby,
Your cradle is pink,
Your dad's unemployed
and too fond of the drink.

Rock a bye baby,
Your cradle is black,
Your daddy's left home
And he's not coming back.

Rock a bye baby,
Your cradle is blue,
Tell me my baby,
What's your mother to do?

ONE DAY SON ALL THIS WILL BE YOURS.

My father died a month ago
And left me all these riches…..
His one glass eye, a piece of pie,
and this large hole in my britches.
(What a start in life, hey?)

HAVE YOU ANY WOOL?

Baa Baa black sheep, have you any wool?
Yes, sir. Yes, Sir. Six bags full.
One for dad's jumper and the baby's hat.
One for gran's cardigan and mum's woolly mat.
One for some ear muffs, for an elephant so big.
With a little bit left over for my bald uncle's wig.
One for a giraffe, for a long necked scarf
And two for the magician –
For the girl he sawed in half.

A STYLISH YOUNG MAN.

A stylish young man in Heckmondwike,
wore trousers which were really too tight,
One day he ate chips,
and heard two large rips,
and giggles from the girls in Heckmondwike.

MEANWHILE IN HALTWHISTLE.

An unfortunate young lady in Haltwhistle,
Screamed "Arrgh!" as she fell in a thistle,
When she cried "ooh!" and "Argh!"
A man from Dunbar,
Came and rescued that girl in Haltwhistle.

P.S . They marry in April!

SLEEPING LIKE A TOP.

My granddad said;
"Don't worry about me. I sleep like a top."
So, last night,
when everyone was sleeping,
I crept into his room to see how tops sleep.
Tops sleep -----------***Noisily!***

MAN IN NUNEATON

There was a young man in Nuneaton,
Who never made note of what he'd eaten.
When they x - rayed his belly,
They found a bike and a telly -
that reckless young man from Nuneaton.

SLOW AND STEADY.

An ambitious young
tortoise from Carlisle,
Bet his friends he could
walk twenty mile.
That was in eighty two,
He's two miles still to do.
But his friends are
all dead in Carlisle!

A MUSICAL AUNT!

Oh so musical is my Auntie Diana,
she is very good on the old piano,
She plays concertos, sonatas and has great fun,
but the shopping and housework,
hardly ever get done – (***according to my mum!)***

STOP PRESS!!

THE OWL AND THE PUSSYCAT (DIDN'T QUITE GET TO SEA).

The owl and the pussycat went to sea,
In a beautiful pea green boat.....
But it was the ***leak inside,***
Which made the owl - ***fly.***
And the pussycat struggle with a - float!

TWINKLE TWINKLE MY CLASS TEACHER.

Twinkle, twinkle, my class teacher,
teaches us English and Computer,
maths and Science, History too.
How she does it all - I haven't a clue!

P.S. Plus geography, R.E. P.E. S.P.E.
and *ad infinitum....* *(Which has now been added to the National Curriculum too!)*
“Oh no ! Not *ad infinitum- as well!”*

ALTERNATIVE VERSION.

Twinkle, twinkle, my class teacher,
Juggles balls and is a fire eater,
Does triple somersaults across the classroom floor,
when we've left school, each night,
at quarter to four.

IN A MINUTE!

Get out of bed and brush your teeth.
In a minute, in a minute
in a minute.
Wash up above and down beneath.
In a minute, in a minute
in a minute.
Put on your clothes and comb your hair.
In a minute, in a minute
in a minute.
Collect your books and come downstairs.
In a minute, in a minute
in a minute.
Eat some toast while you watch T.V.
In a minute, in a minute
in a minute.
Cereal and a cup of tea.
In a minute, in a minute
in a minute.
Grab your school bag, gloves and scarf.
In a minute, in a minute
in a minute.
Put on your coat, leap in the car.
In a minute, in a minute
in a minute.
Drive to school, must not be late.
In a minute, in a minute,

in a minute.
The National Curriculum cannot wait!
In a minute, in a minute, in a minute.
No! Not in a minute - ***now!***

THE OLD NAMES.

Lots of eager year ones sitting in row,
One called Joshua and two called Joe.
Three called Jordan and four called Jack.
It's funny how the old names keep coming back.

GOOD! BUT NOT THAT GOOD.

I am very good at my A, B, C.
I just get stuck ……….
When I get to ………..D!

One, Two, Three, Four,
…………………………… Nine!
My counting's
Improving –
all the time.

One add two,
is so easy for me.
But six add seven,
Is………………***still a ……..mystery!***

NATHANIEL KNOX.

Nathaniel Knox, Nathaniel Knox,
Nathaniel Knox, has outrageous socks.
He wears them in the bath.
He wears them in his bed
and sometimes for a laugh,
he wears them on his head!
He dangles them like ear rings,
hanging from his ears.
He even wears them on his nose
when full of Christmas cheers.
He often wears an odd pair,
like one purple and one blue.
Sometimes without thinking,
He pulls them over shoes.
He wears stripy ones and zigzag ones
and ones with lots of spots.

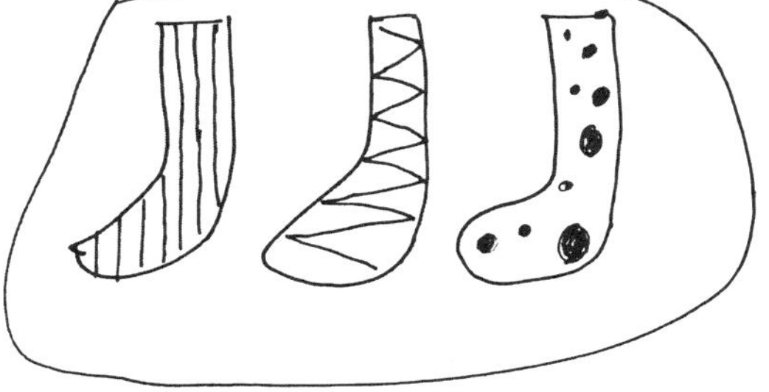

There are droopy ones and Snoopy ones
and ones with polka dots.

There are some with Mickey Mouse on
and some with Donald Duck.
Some that you can drink out of
and some that you can suck.
There's a pair made out of chocolate
and one of marzipan.
There are some you'd like to nibble -
and some of them you can!

You never know the socks,
Nathaniel Knox, is pulling on.
(Some will ring a bell for you
and some will ding a gong!)
Some of them blow raspberries
and some will play a tune
and one pair takes to howling
at the sight of a full moon!

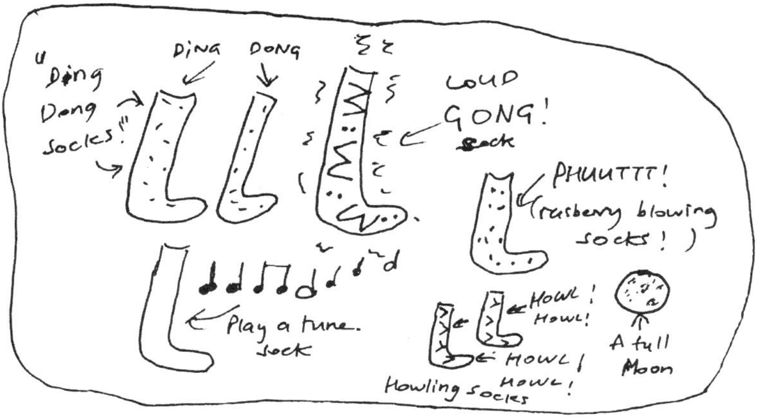

There are orange ones and lemon ones
and those with stripes or hoops.
There are some that taste of porridge
and some that taste of soup.
People suddenly sniff the air
and say that pong smells kind of homely.
He'll tell them that it's chicken or maybe
minestrone.

Nathaniel is a bank manager,
He takes the tube each day.

He wears a pin striped suit,
He looks sober, staid and grey.
But beneath the suit of Nathaniel Knox
there lies a man with outrageous socks!
Nathaniel Knox, Nathaniel Knox,
Nathaniel Knox, has outrageous socks.

TWINKLE TWINKLE FUNNY CLOWN.

Twinkle, Twinkle, funny clown,
throws three balls up and only two come down.
Large red nose and huge bow tie,
for squirting water in your eye.
Custard pies thrown in his face
or down baggy trousers
round his waist.
He'll ride a trick bike,
then fall off – Splat!
He's a juggler,
comedian
and acrobat!

A WELL ORDERED LIFE.

A ninety year old in The Borders
had a life which was very well ordered.
Each morning at six,
He'd do cart-wheeling tricks,
Then yell rude remarks at his warders.

He would bathe every morning at nine,
in two feet of Blueberry wine.
When his pink skin turned blue,
it raised an eyebrow or two,
But he said; "It's the wine! Hic! I'm fine!"

Each afternoon, he'd dig a few holes.
If folks asked him why, he'd say; "Moles!"
Then he'd produce two sky rockets
From out of his pockets
and tie them to the end of two poles.

When asked;
"Have the things ever flown?   He'd reply;
"Why of course, they're well known.
They travel to Mars,
turn round at the stars,
stop somewhere for lunch,
then come home."

This eccentric old man
From The Borders,
with a life so unusual, but ordered.
goes to bed promptly at ten,
on the stroke of Big Ben -
to the blessed relief of his warders.

ALL ABOUT THE PORK PIE.

The pork pie is a crusty fish.
It swims about in jelly.
It likes to sit with pickled friends,
when football's on the telly.

THE WING COMMANDER.

A strange wing commander in the force,
sat down for lunch with a horse,
He said; "By golly! She can eat!
What a fantastical feat!
She's just finished her twenty third course!"

BATH NIGHT IN BUDE.

There was a charming young lady in Bude,
took a bath as you do, in the nude.
But round about ten,
Some women and men,
came up through the plughole for food.
("Excuse me, is this the Chinese restaurant?"
"No! It's ***my*** bathroom - get out at once!"
"Oh sorry! Wrong address!")

MY BABY BROTHER.

My baby brother drives me mad,
His noises are rude and his smells are bad.
I love him yes, but I cannot pretend,
To like the mess he makes at either end!

EATING OUT.

My dad told me that we were
going to eat out at Alfrescos.
I thought, wow! Great!
An – ***Italian restaurant.***
But he must have changed his mind,
Because we just had a barbeque
In the garden instead - ***Burnt sausages again!***

NOT THIS MAN'S BEST FRIEND!

There was an old man in Nantucket,
Whose false leg fell off in a bucket.
Though not in the habit,
he reached out to grab it,
But a Dalmatian raced by and then took it!

(Hey you! That's my leg you've just stolen !
Bring it back here at once! I'm playing left back for Nantucket Rovers Reserves tomorrow!")
P.S. Where is Nantucket?
P.S.S. Does he look like a Nantucket Rovers Reserve? Star player? (I thought not!)
He'll have to miss a match or two – methinks!!

A SKYE BOAT SONG?

A sweet young lassie from Skye,
smiled as she ate a meat pie,
but inside a male choir,
sang songs ever higher,
which quickly brought tears to her eyes!

A POLITICAL ANIMAL.

Don't ask me about politics
And all that sort of stuff,
I have the same opinions - as my dog -
Wuff! Wuff! Wuff!

THE STRANGEST THING I EVER DID SEE.

The strangest thing I ever did see,
Was a gorilla on a bicycle on the M3.
taking over all the cars in the fast lane,
wearing cowboy boots and a cowboy hat
and what was also strange – were the strange
flowery glasses and the lipstick he wore.
And the way he waved as he reached - *ninety four!!!!*

THE NEXT STRANGEST THING...

The next strangest thing I ever did see was -
six monkeys at a bus stop wearing bikinis.
Four on guitars and one on the drums
and one on a pair of stilts doing his sums!
What tune were they playing?
I don't know, since you've asked.
But all the people in cars,
laughed as they passed.

ALL ABOUT THE SAUSAGE.

The sausage
is a cunning bird,
It wears
a woolly hat.
It makes a
funny sizzling sound,
When laying
on its back.

JENNIFER JONES.

Jennifer Jones, Jennifer Jones,
Spends all her time on mobile phones,
rings her friends with great persistence.
What did we do before their existence?

UNUSUAL GROWTH.

There was a
very tall man
in Bengal,
Who grew
more
than twenty
feet tall.
Folks were
heard to laugh,
When he looked
down on giraffes,
that incredibly
tall man
from Bengal.

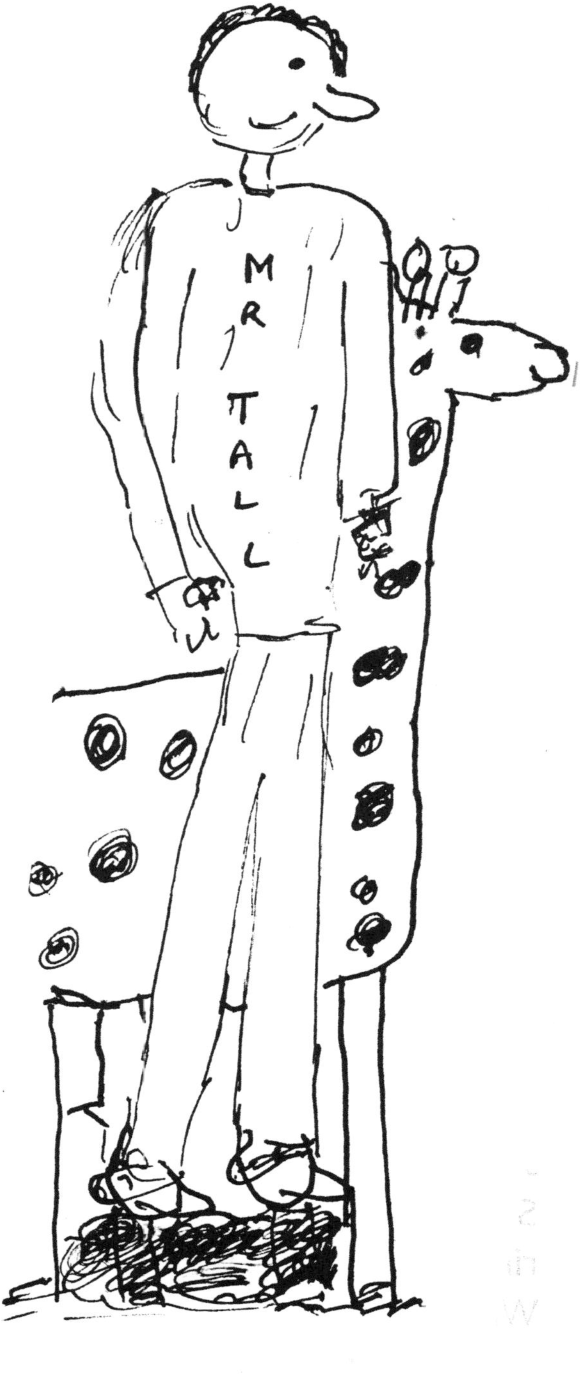

A LONG NOSE IN MELROSE.

A remarkable man in Melrose,
Had an amazingly
long rounded nose,
When folks stopped to stare,
He stuck his nose in the air - and said;
"You should see the length of my toes!"

HEAVY DRINKING.

There was an odd man in Somerset,
Who swallowed a pond for a bet.
It was just his bad luck,
that he swallowed four ducks
and was heard to - "quack, quack" at the vets.

MEANWHILE IN BYRNESS.

A Pennine Way walker, near Bryness,
saw a huge incredible nest.
It was ***two metre wide,***
with hammering inside,
which caused him to flee – with ***great zest! Arrggh!***

A SANDWICH IN NANTWICH.

An inquisitive young man in Nantwich,
heard noises inside his sandwich.
He saw a tiny brass band,
with instruments in hand,
Going Ompah! Pah, pah ! in his sandwich!

A SUDDEN MOVEMENT IN THE REPTILE POOL.

The crocodile lay as still as a tree,
though his roving eyes were following me.
Then his mouth opened wide,
Revealing - ***teeth!***

I'm glad I'm - UP ABOVE -
and he's down - BENEATH!

A LADY OF DUNOON.

An impulsive young lady from Dunoon,
awoke to find a horse in her room.
The horse said -
"Last night in underwear,
You rode me upstairs.
You did it for a bet - I presume?"

A TIGER'S ADVICE TO HIS KEEPER.

"Tiger, tiger, burning bright,
what will you have for dinner tonight?"
"The usual menu, a steak or two,
But if you get too near, I may eat -***you!"***

A VERY STRANGE TALE.

There was a large, bull frog,
And a huge bull dog,
sitting on a log - by the sea.
When the dog and the frog,
Were joined by a mog,
a mog and a hog, who'd come for tea.
But then the frog and the dog,
And the mog and the hog,
were suddenly agog,
when out of the bog – with a smile -
leapt the most gigantic crocodile!
And the crocodile said;
"Am I too late,
for the buns and the cake
and the juice and the jelly- and the cream?"
"No, no!" said the dog and the frog,
and the mog. "You're just in time,"

said the hog, "for the feast!"
So, the dog and the frog
and the mog and the hog
sat down on the log and ate.
While the croc from the bog,
Joined them on the log
and was glad that he wasn't -
too late.

MY PET GIRAFFE.

I have a pet giraffe called George.
I take him everywhere.
When I walk along the high street,
you should see the people stare.
They turn to look and how they talk.
at the sight of a boy, taking his giraffe for a walk.
They laugh and hoot, make silly remarks,
but George and I don't care,
Just to see their shocked and startled faces
makes it worth just being there.
Sometimes on hearing their laughter,
George stares down and cranes his neck
and he whispers in my ear,
"To what do they object?
Do you think it's my choice of hat,
with the flowers around the brim?

Or maybe it's the frilly knickers I wear,
with their gold and lacy trim?
Or maybe it's the long silk stockings
Which stretch down to my red, walking boots?"
"No. It's that long, green, luminous scarf you wear,"
I tell him. "But who really gives a hoot?"
"Well, I Don't!" George whispers,
As we continue down that street.

My ***four metre high pet Giraffe - and me!***

GIGGLE GLASSES.

I bought these special glasses with their fantastic magic glazing.
The things you see with them, are truly quite amazing.
They call them ***giggle glasses,*** because that is what you do,
when you place them on your ears, you laugh and titter too!

Well, I never did! Look! Way up in the sky,
six pigs pass in formation,
Grunting loudly, flying by!

And Look! Now there are penguins on motor bikes,
speeding fast and four abreast
and they are wearing leather jackets
with "hell's penguins" on the chest.

There's a hippo driving a taxi.
There's an elephant wearing skates.
There's an alligator playing the piano
and a polar bear juggling with crates!

There's a giraffe wearing a leotard,
Dancing with a frog! What a caper!

There's a baboon eating ice cream
and an orang-utan reading the paper.

There's a lion on a skateboard.
There's a mouse selling cheese.
While a chimpanzee and an emu
Have just hurtled passed on skis!

There is a rhinoceros on a pogo stick.
There is a crocodile on a scooter.
There are three pelicans in the sandpit
and two pandas on computer.

Well, I never did!
It's amazing lads and lasses.
What fantastic things you'll see,
when you're wearing – ***"giggle glasses."***

NOBODY'S BETTER THAN ME!

Nobody's better at breast stroke
and it's the races today.
Nobody's better at front crawl
So, I'm so glad
that nobody's away!

(because I'm the
second best
after - ***him!)***

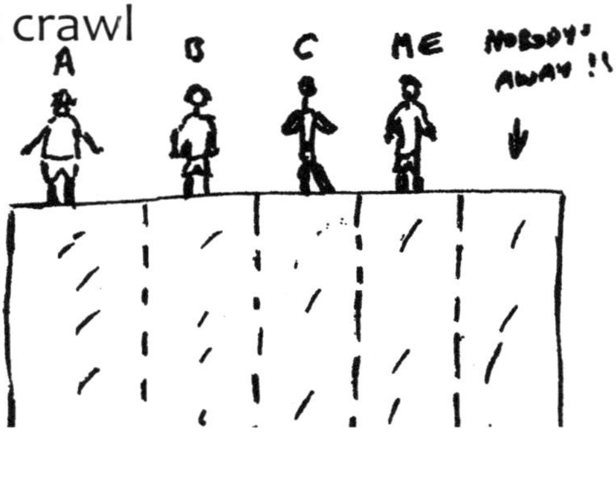

PARTY ANIMALS.

Theme parties for birthdays are really quite the thing.
And I ***did*** want my party to go with a zing.
So I invited many friends, from the local zoo.
They're really ***party animals*** so they knew just what to do.
They were baboons with balloons,
in polka dotted pantaloons.
They were two kind old rhinos, dancing on the lino.
They were giraffes full of laughter,
reaching to the rafters.
There was an iguana, from French Guyana,
playing the grand piano!
While a gnu and a kangaroo, waited in the loo queue.
There was a bulldozer and a cowdozer,
snoozing on the softest sofa.
There was a parrot and a jackdaw,
skating on the parquet floor.
There was a white horse, who of course,
ate ice cream with chocolate sauce.
While a dish of lemon meringue,
proved a hit with the orang-utans.
There were chimpanzees, with hairy knees,
swinging from the high trapeze.

(Well, the chandelier.)
While penguins, with cheeky grins,
filled the bath and then jumped in.
There was an aardvark, and a basking shark,
dancing in the semi dark. (How lovely!)
There was a hippo and a hippo-ess,
who amused the guests by playing chess.
There was a polar bear, in a high backed chair,
who was gently combing, granny's hair.
(oh, how she loved it!)
There was a blue whale and his pink whale wife,
who had just swam in, from a firth near Fife.
Then the elephants in spotted pants,
sang for me, their birthday chants.
(six verses - how divine!)
Then a jagu***ar***, played a mean guit***ar,***
And everyone sang an ***opera.***
(Well, a short song!)
What a memorable birthday.
Apart from all the mess!
I wonder what birthday theme,
I'll dream up next?

LITTLE FROG.

Twinkle, twinkle
little frog,
Why are you sitting
on a sausage dog?
And why is it driving
a motor bike?
Twinkle, twinkle –
what are you like?

THIS CHARMING MAN.

Terence McDiddler,
The three stringed fiddler,
Could charm if you please,
the fish from the seas.
But he doesn't charm the ladies,
To them he's a miss,
They're not keen
on the fiddle
or the constant
smell of fish.

Pooo! Poooo!

GUITAR MAN.

When I play my guitar I feel really cool.
But I end up feeling an idiot and a bit of a fool.
Twinkle, twinkle and a hey! diddle diddle!
My plectrum is lost in that hole in the middle.

BONGO BANGING!

Tum, tum, tum,
I banged the bongo,
With my dog whose
name is Pongo.
But Pongo banged too
loud and blew it!
Now my mum won't
let us do it!

TWINKLE TWINKLE LITTLE STAR.

Twinkle twinkle little star,
How well you play your rock guitar.
Twang, twang, twang
and strum, strum, strum.
A huge rock star –
at five foot one!

SPORTING HORSE.

Twinkle, twinkle little horse,
What are you doing on my golf course?
And how did you manage that hole in one?
I've been trying for years and it can't be done!

SPORTING COW.

Twinkle, twinkle little cow,
How you scored that goal I can't guess how.
A thirty yard volley! How do you shoot that far?
They'd show countless replays, if you were a
Premier league star!
PS in fact, bearing in mind you're a cow – scoring
goals like that would be shown countless times on
"You Tube!"
If only someone other than me had seen it!!!!!!!

YOUR WORST NIGHTMARE

Twinkle, twinkle, centipede,
swallowed a packet of sunflower seeds.
Now the monster creeping up your hall,
has one hundred legs and is – ***ten feet tall!!***
Arrrggh!!

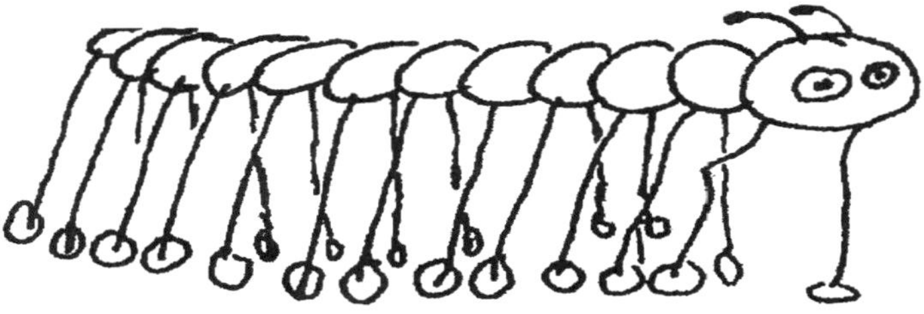

DAREDEVIL TOAD.

Twinkle, twinkle, daredevil toad,
took up pole vaulting over busy roads.
The M1 motorway is his best leap so far.
Where he vaulted four juggernauts, a bus and a car!

REVERTING TO TYPE.

Twinkle, twinkle little goat,
Sailed the Atlantic in a rowing boat,
When the reporter's asked the goat,
"How was it for you?"
The goat ate their notebooks and their pencils too!

EXTRA! EXTRA! PIG SWIMS CHANNEL.

Twinkle, twinkle magnificent pig,
Swam the channel in a curly wig,
From Calais to Dover,
where the pig, did a jig.
The fastest swim ever –
For a pig with a wig!

LOOKING THROUGH WINDOWS.

A cat looked through the window and saw
herself chasing next door's big fat bulldog.
A mischievous dog looked through the window
and saw his owner being groomed for a 'Human
show'.
A carrot looked through the window and saw
himself crunching on a tasty rabbit.
A strawberry looked through the window
And saw himself at Wimbledon
eating a tennis player with fresh dairy cream.
A rabbit looked through the window and saw
herself shooting at a farmer.
A young lamb looked through the window and saw
himself eating a juicy rack of human with
mint sauce!
The dog looked through
the window again and
finally got his owner
to sit when he was told!

SOME OF PROFESSOR SIDNEY BARNACLES MOST USELESS INVENTIONS... SO FAR!

1. A pair of one legged tights.
2 A pair of no legged trousers.
3. An eraser which fiendishly only rubs out on days without a y in them.
4. A pencil sharpener which only sharpens unleaded pencils.
5. A kettle which boils in twenty seconds - and doesn't need water!
6. A musical instrument which only plays one note - badly.
7. A blackboard which can be written on only by teacher's who are ten or younger.
8. Revolving school dinner tables to make dinner times at school much more fun.
9. Cardboard cricket bats for an easier swing.
10. Robotic footballs which when kicked go - ***where they want to go!***
11. A lift which only goes down!
12. A room with only one door - in the ceiling.
13. A helter skelter with no steps up to the top.
14. Square car wheels, triangular bus wheels and rectangular lorry wheels!
15. Traffic lights which are ***red*** all day in

every direction. (Or better still- ***green*** in every direction!)

16. A new road system - where all cars drive on the left, lorries on the right and buses drive on the left ***and*** on the right hand side of the road – to speed up public transport!
17. And finally - a poet's nightmare - a poem with no words.

ALLITERATION WITH NUMBERS.

One weighty walrus waved a wonky wand at watching wavers.
Two teething tortoises tore a terrible tear in ten tall tulips.
Three thoughtful fellows threw out three thirsty thieves on Thursday.
Four flaming forest fires finally fizzled out on Friday.
Five foreign fellows had a frenzied feast of fine food at Freddie's friendly farmhouse.
Six steaming saucepans sizzled on Sally Shackelton's stove.

One weighty Walrus waving his wonky wand!

Seven sneering savages sipped cider
while Susie Sweeney sizzled.
Eight earnest elephants easily ate
eleven Easter eggs each.
Nine terrible Tyrannosauruses tore with tearing,
tortuous teeth at Tiny Terry Thompson's teddy
bear.

THE MERMAID.

I was floating on my lilo bed,
when with tired eyes, I raised my head.
I saw something which gave me such a shock.
A mermaid perched on a nearby rock.
I rubbed my eyes and took a second look,
saw the mermaid was reading a picture book.
"I am reading about human children," she said,
"Perhaps you can assist.
Do you think that human children,
really do exist?"
I laughed and said; "Why of course they do.
In fact, dear mermaid, I am one too!"
At that, I pointed to my legs
and flapped them up and down.
"It must be difficult swimming around with those!"
She said, with a mermaid's frown.
Then she beckoned for me to follow her,
and I swam to the bottom of the sea,
with the mermaid holding onto my hand,
we headed to her house for tea.
We had clams and oysters and seaweed soup
and we talked like we were friends.
And we swam around, met lots of fish,
And I wished my trip would not end.

Never once did I get out of breath,
as I swam with my mermaid girl.
In fact, I found I could talk, as we swam,
It seemed the most natural thing in the world.
Then she gave me a pearl, this beautiful mermaid,
And turned to me and said,
"Please come back and visit me again dear friend."
And I awoke on my lilo bed.

BIG MAC. (THE GIGANTIC GIANT).

Dinosaur sized.
He is as tall as a block of flats,
as wide as a row of terrace houses.
Huge, red eyes which light up like two
fire engines on their way to a fire.
Jet black, pointed teeth,
in a mouth as vast and cavernous as a cave.
He has tree trunk legs. Muscles like hillocks.
Heavy metal roar! Brass band snore!
He's as strong as a chieftain tank
and charges like a herd of rhinos.
But he's as lazy as a pride of lions,
in the hot, midday sun.
He's nasty when angry, though ***soft*** at times.
When picking up a rose he goes - "Aw!"

But he could flatten a supermarket, crush up a house, demolish a bus shelter - with one kick.
I'm glad he's my friend.
He comes round for snacks -
tea and crumpets - for my friend- 'Big Mac.'

A RECIPE TO MAKE A PERFECT DRAGON.

To make a perfect dragon -
Take the hottest coal from the fire.
From China - a fire cracker!
Add the hottest chillies from Mexico
and sizzling curries from India.
Mix in white hot, Sahara desert sand
and sumptuous sauces from Africa
and spices from the Orient.

Take a chieftain tank from America
then place them in a cauldron.
Add a Pterodactyl's wings,
A crocodile's scaly skin,
A T- Rex's roar, a tiger's stripes and the brightest rainbow from the sky.
Stir in two buckets of exploding,
freshly erupted volcano
and bubbling water from a hot spring.
Mix for three hours. Place on a plate.
Wait to cool. Hey presto!
You will have...... the perfect dragon.

WHAT GOES ON IN A CAT'S HEAD?

What goes on in a cat's head?
Well, in this cat's head,
there is a box to sleep in,
a chair to hide under,
a window to stare out from,
a bedroom to sneak into when no one is around,
a garage roof to sit on top of,
a warm cosy place in the garden
and a tree to sit in whilst waiting for the birds.

What else is in a cat's head?
Well, there is a mouse to chase, small and white
and furry.
There is a ball to dribble round the room.
There is some silver paper, wrapped up as a ball,
to knock under the settee.
There is a favourite knee to lay on,
a favourite food to eat -
(salmon and trout in a prawn sauce).

What else is in this cat's head?
There is a new kind of purr he hasn't perfected yet.
There is a new kind of food he hasn't tasted yet.
There is a new kind of cream he hasn't sipped yet.
And there are several parts of his body he hasn't

licked today-yet.
There are dozens of cosy places in the house
and garden he hasn't fully explored yet.
There is a new sort of exam all cat owners
must take, which he hasn't written yet.
But it is called; "How to be the perfect owner of
cats!"
Now, that will be some test to take.

THE FAMILY ARE NOT AT HOME.

Hey diddle, diddle,
Two cats play the fiddles,
While the dog plays a mean saxophone.
While the rabbits in the yard,
bang their bongos very hard,
when the family are not at home.

All the birds up on the roof,
are tooting on their flutes,
while the pigeons play their slide trombones.
And elsewhere the budgerigars,
are all twanging their guitars,
when the family are not at home.

The goldfish stop their swimming,
for a spot of hand bell ringing,
while the gerbil plays a tiny xylophone.
And the mice are dancing tap,
while the hamsters love to rap,
when the family are not at home.

Bing bong, ping poot,
Twiddly dido, diddly hoot,
The family are not at home.
Yahoo!
The family are not at home.
Hee Hah!
The family are not at home.

SO, WHAT!

So, you're much bigger than me.
So, what!
So, you're far stronger I am.
So, what!
So, you're more muscular than I am.
So, what!
So, you've got sharper claws.
So, what!
So, you've got longer, sharper teeth.
So, what!
So, you can make a lot more noise than I can!
So, what!
So, you're a - ***meat eating dinosaur!***
So, wh….Fancy a crisp?

SIDNEY THE SPIDER.

Sidney the spider runs along your hall,
hairy, black and scary, but only very small.
With his eight long legs, he strides across the floor.
With his two beady eyes fixed on your bedroom door.
Sidney the spider scales your bedroom walls,
hairy, black and scary, but only very small.
Sidney the spider, is high above your bed,
hanging from the ceiling, dangling by a thread.
Sidney the spider has decided to drop down.
Winding on his rope like thread,
He falls, on your dressing gown.
He hears screaming. He hears screeching.
That's you - yelling for your - ***mum!***
And Sidney with his eight legs
now decides to run.
This scary creature scarpers,
what else can he do?
He's seen and heard this monster
And that monster is - ***you!***
Sidney tells his wife Simone.
"It was like a bad, bad dream.
I heard this huge and noisy monster.
The worst I've ever seen!"
Sidney the spider, tries to close his eyes,

but he sees this monster in his head,
one thousand times his size.
This scary creature curls up,
What else can he do?
There's a monster in his head -
And that monster is - YOU!!!!

THE WINCEY FAMILY OUTING.

Incey Wincey spider,
climbing up the spout.
Followed by his brother,
the one whose got the gout.
Followed by his sisters,
Dawn, Diane and Dee.
Arriving up the plughole,
To scare my family!
Aarrgh!
(But they don't scare me of course!)

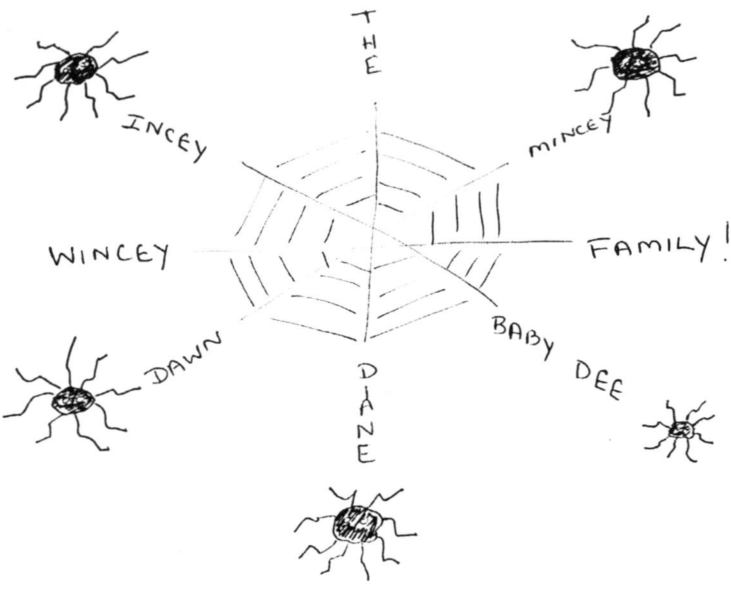

WHEN BILLY GOT EATEN BY A CROCODILE.

When Billy got eaten by a crocodile,
The villagers were terribly cross.
"What's a crocodile doing in the village pond?"
They cried.
And the crocodile confessed.
"I was lost. I saw a sign which said,
'right to Chipping Sodbury,
and left to the blue river Nile.'
But since I couldn't read a word of it,
I've ended up here for a while."
"You can't stay here!" said the villagers.
"Not now young Billy's been eaten."
And the crocodile said;
"Okay, fair enough!"
And now he's in Norway - or Sweden.

THE LION'S RAP.

I saw this six foot lion,
prowling in his cage.
When he saw me, he roared,
But he wasn't in a rage.
He said; "I'm fed up of being miserable,
so I want to make it clear,
I'm going to do something useful,
while I'm stuck in here!"
He said; "I'm going to write a rap.
Then I'm going to dance the tap.
I may just do a jigsaw.
Then lay down and have a nap.
I may just write a book,
about the African plains.
I've never actually been there,
But you'll not hear me complain.
Here they throw my meals in.
Three good meals a day.
I don't have to chase or kill anything,
and they serve it on a tray.
Yes, I'm going to write a rap.
Then I'll learn to dance the tap.
I may do 'The Times crossword,'
before a game of snap!
I'll learn to play the cello,

Or maybe the violin,
I haven't got the instruments,
But I'm sure they'll send some in!
Here, they never shoot to kill me.
I never need run for my life.
Though I hate the grinning public
Who stare and give me strife.
For them I think I'll - ***ROAR!***
Then I'll ***roar*** some more!
And then maybe for an encore,
I'll roll round on the floor.
I'll let my keeper tickle me,
while I try a gentle -***purr,***
as he runs his hands so gently,
down my amazing mane and fur.
Then later, I'll write that book
About the African plains,
As I said, I've never been there,
But you'll not hear me complain.
Then I'm going to write a rap,
Then maybe dance the tap.
I may even take up painting,
done by numbers on my lap!
I'm fed up of being miserable
And I want to make it clear,
I'm going to do something useful,
while I'm stuck in here.

while I'm stuck... while I'm stuck..
while I'm stuck in here!

THERE'S TROUBLE AT THE ZOO.

Hee by gum and tickety boo,
I hear that there's trouble, down at the zoo.

The monkeys are revolting, wear potties on their heads.
While banging on their bongos, and they will not go to bed.
The lions in their cages, try break dancing and rap.
The flamingos in the pink, prefer to tango and to tap.
Hee by gum and tickety boo,
I believe that there's trouble, down at the zoo.

The elephants are perfecting kangaroo hops.
But don't get below, when an elephant drops.
The emus amaze, by flying in the sky,
And they haven't done that, since the queen was -
this high!

Hee by gum and tickety boo,
By crikey! There's trouble, down at the zoo.

The gorillas have formed an animal choir.
They sing the low notes, the giraffes sing much
higher.
The rhinos present their own ballet each night.
Swan Lake done by rhinos is a frightening sight.

Hee by gum and tickety boo,
By golly! There's trouble, down at the zoo.

The baboons, well bless 'em, love a bit of fun,
so they hang upside down and stick out their bums!
(sophisticated stuff!)
The pandas don't like it, it's really not their scene,
so they are sitting in the corner,
knitting something quite obscene!

Hee by gum and tickety boo,
By George! There's trouble, down at the zoo.

Hee by gum! By crikey!
By golly! By George! And tickety boo!
By heck! There's trouble, down at the zoo!

SEVEN LITTLE MONKEYS.

Seven little monkeys, swinging in their cage,
one got an offer, to write a monkey problem page.
Six little monkeys, swinging from bar to bar,
One signed a contract, to be a T.V. star.
Five little monkeys, swinging upside down,
One left in a business suit, for a meeting in the town.
Four little monkeys, swinging from tree to tree,
One left to write a book, on monkey history.
Three little monkeys, hanging on a branch,
One left for Texas, to start a cattle ranch.
Two little monkeys, swinging from tyre to tyre,
One left for the circus, to balance on high wire.
One little monkey, feeling all alone,
missed the other monkeys, so was always on the phone.

A NOTE ON ETIQUETTE.

Never play snap with a crocodile
And never play cards with a shark.

Never play rugby with a rhino
Or invite vampires home after dark.
Never try boxing a kangaroo
Or challenge a cheetah to a race.
And never, ever invite chimpanzees back for tea,
because their manners are a terrible disgrace.

A MEAL DEAL.

There was a young lady on castors,
Who smiled as she rode ever faster,
She came to a stop, in a Cannibal's pot.
And they seasoned her ready for afters!

A LEAK IN THE HEAD.

I had just finished an hour long performance
Of poetry in a junior school
in front of 450 children.
Afterwards, I was perspiring profusely.
As I walked down the school corridor,
a little boy, stared up at me rather puzzled.
He pointed at my, soaking wet hair,
And said; "Mr! have you got a ***leak in the head?"***
"Yes!" I replied laughing loudly.
"I suppose I must have!"

MEANWHILE IN ANOTHER SCHOOL.

Meanwhile in another school, a child of about the same age, greeted me in the corridor,
with the phrase -"Hey, Mr! You're a great **Poemer** you!"
"Thankyou." I replied, pleased to be – "A great - ***poemer!"***

DIPLODOCUS DAYDREAMS.

The teacher was at the blackboard,
teaching us some maths.
And the hands of the clock
were not moving very fast.
So, I glanced out of the window,
just as a dinosaur strolled passed.
It was only for a second,
Then the dinosaur was - gone.
No one else seemed to notice,
D I P - L O - DO - C U S,
So, the maths lesson
went on!!!!

AN AMAZING TALENT.

A remarkable pair of baboons,
Read the financial pages each noon.
They bought and sold shares,
became ***baboonianaires.***
Now they're planning a world cruise in June.

JUMPING JELLYBEANS -FLYING BULLS!

As I was walking peacefully by,
I saw a bull fly in the sky.
Unless my eyes were seeing things,
This flying bull had tiny wings!
It landed in a nearby tree
and then proceeded to sing to me.
The bull sang sweetly, you have my word.
But then – the ***bull finch –*** is a bonny ***bird.***

IF NOBODY SANG.

If nobody sang
and nobody tried,
if nobody laughed
and nobody cried.
If the grass stopped growing
and the forests DIS A PP EAR ED
And the ozone layer
proved worst than we feared.
If the mountains
C
R
U
M
B
L
E
D
And filled up the sea.

Will you *still come round - for crumpets and tea?*